OUT IN SPAC

C000149056

What's inside?

Where we live

Space is so enormous that it's hard to imagine. It's like a giant city with different neighbourhoods. Our home, planet Earth, is in a neighbourhood called the solar system. The Earth shares the solar system with other planets, meteors, comets, asteroids, moons and the Sun.

the Moon

meteor

2

comet

planet Mercury

planet Venus

planet Earth

asteroid

the Sun is a star

3

The Sun

The Sun is the nearest star to Earth. Like all stars, it's a blazing ball of fire. The Sun gives us light and keeps us warm. Without it, the Earth would be dark and freezing cold. The Sun is at the centre of the solar system.

How bright?

The Sun is too bright for our eyes, so never look at it directly, even with sunglasses. Protect your body, too. Always wear a hat, shirt and sunblock.

Sun facts

From Earth, the Sun looks huge. But if you stood on the faraway planet Pluto, it would look just like a bright star in the night sky.

Both the ancient Greeks and Romans believed that the Sun was a powerful god driving his chariot across the sky.

The Sun is so far away that it would take 20 years for an aeroplane to fly there.

Planets

There are nine planets in our solar system and they're all different. Some are sizzling hot, others are icy cold. The smaller planets are mostly hard and rocky. The bigger planets are covered with thick, soupy clouds of gas.

poisonous Venus

Venus is our nearest neighbour. It's scorching hot and covered with poisonous clouds.

rocky Mercury

Mercury is a bare, rocky world. At night, it's freezing cold, but during the day, it's baking hot.

watery Earth

From space, the Earth is a beautiful blue-and-white ball. Most of its surface is covered with water.

dusty Mars

Mars is a dry, dusty planet. It has volcanoes, but they're dead and don't erupt any more.

giant Jupiter

Jupiter is the biggest planet. Its surface is covered with red and yellow clouds.

topsy-turvy Uranus

Uranus is the only planet that spins round on its side. It's a dark, frozen world far from the Sun.

swirly Saturn

Saturn has bright, swirling rings that make it easy to recognize. It's a cold, windy place with many moons.

windy Neptune

Neptune is a stormy planet. It has the strongest winds in the solar system.

tiny Pluto

Pluto is the smallest planet in the solar system. It's the furthest planet from the Sun.

The Earth

The Earth is a special planet because it has water and air. As far as we know, it's the only place where animals live. The Earth spins like a top. It takes one day, or 24 hours, to spin round once. The Earth also travels round the Sun. It takes one year, or 365 days, to travel round the Sun once.

How fast?

The Earth zooms round the Sun really quickly. You don't notice it, but the ground beneath your feet races along faster than a jumbo jet!

Earth facts

As the
Earth spins,
different parts of it
move into the Sun's light.
When the part of the
world where you live faces
the Sun, it's daytime. When it faces
away from the Sun, it's night-time.

The Earth's surface
is mostly water.
Imagine the Earth
as a cake – only
a small slice
would be land,
the rest would
be water!

Many years ago, people thought
that the Earth was flat and that
you'd fall off the edge if
you travelled
too far!

9

Shooting across space

Have you ever seen a bright spark of light shooting across the sky like a firework? That's a meteor! And if you're lucky, you may spot a comet too. Look out for a long cloudy streak of light moving slowly through the sky.

meteor

Sometimes, a small chunk of space rock or dust shoots towards the Earth. When it burns up in the sky, it's called a meteor or shooting star.

comet

A comet is a dusty, rocky snowball. We see it only when it passes close by the Sun. Some of the icy comet melts and leaves a huge snowy cloud trailing behind.

asteroid

An asteroid is a lump of rock spinning in space. It can be as small as a pebble or bigger than a house.

Dinosaur disaster

A few scientists believe the dinosaurs died out when an asteroid crashed into Earth. The crash made a dust cloud that blocked out the Sun. Without sunlight, plants couldn't grow and the dinosaurs had no food.

Our Moon

The Moon is our next-door neighbour and it travels round the Earth. The Moon is a dry dusty ball of rock where nothing grows. It can be very hot in the day and very cold at night. The sky around it is always pitch black.

How quiet?

There isn't any air on the Moon to carry sounds. This means that even if you banged drums as loudly as you could, you wouldn't make any noise.

ha ha
Where do astronauts go to study?
Mooniversity!

There isn't any wind or rain on the Moon, so footprints made by the astronaut Neil Armstrong in 1969 are still there!

The Moon looks different each night. Sometimes, it's a round ball. Other times, it's a crescent shape or it even disappears completely.

If the Moon floated down to Earth, it would be just the right size to sit on a piece of land as big as Australia.

3, 2, 1... Blast off!

In 1969, a giant rocket called Saturn 5 blasted off into space, carrying astronauts to the Moon. Two astronauts, Neil Armstrong and Edwin 'Buzz' Aldrin, became the first men ever to walk on the Moon. The astronauts landed back on Earth safely after a journey that lasted eight days.

Saturn 5

When Saturn 5 blasted into space, it was travelling 70 times faster than a car on a motorway.

Guess what?
The engines of the Saturn 5 rocket were as powerful as 30 jumbo-jet engines.

The moon lander was stored in here.

Astronauts sat in here.

Moon lander

The astronauts flew down to the Moon in the Apollo 11 moon lander. They explored the surface and planted a flag that's still there today.

Giant rocket

Saturn 5 was 111 metres tall. That's even taller than the Statue of Liberty!

UNITED STATES

Living in space

When astronauts go into space, they take food, air and water with them. They also take books to read and games to play. In space, everything floats around, so one game astronauts can't play is tennis. The ball would just fly away!

Spacesuit

When astronauts leave their spacecraft, they wear suits that have an air supply so that they can breathe. The bulky suit also protects the person inside from the heat and cold outside.

Space food

At meal times, astronauts strap their food trays to their legs, to stop the trays from floating away. The food is sticky or stuck on to spikes, to stop it from drifting off as well.

Guess what?
In a space toilet, astronauts sit on funnels that suck away all the waste.

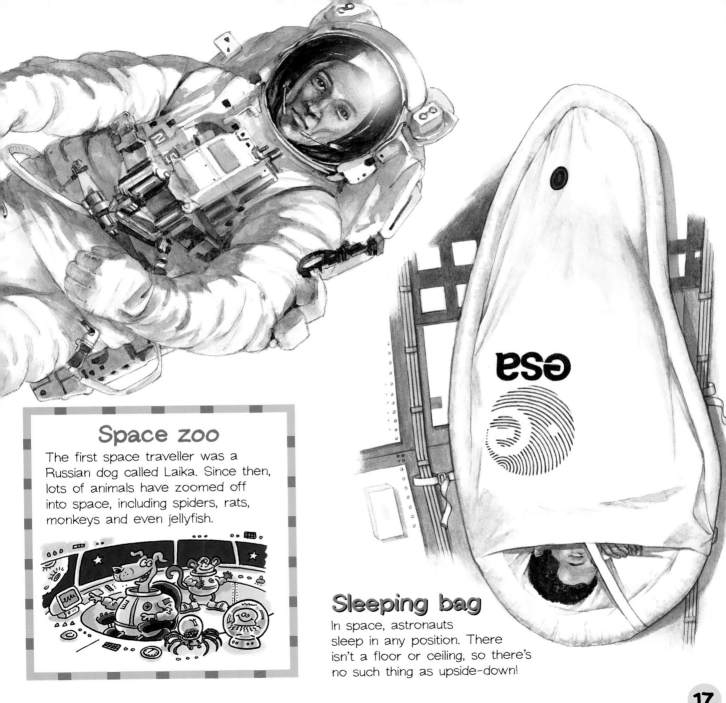

Space zoo

The first space traveller was a Russian dog called Laika. Since then, lots of animals have zoomed off into space, including spiders, rats, monkeys and even jellyfish.

Sleeping bag

In space, astronauts sleep in any position. There isn't a floor or ceiling, so there's no such thing as upside-down!

esa

Do you believe in aliens?

There are lots of films and books about aliens. But do they really exist? Let's try to find out...

1 I've heard that people have seen alien spaceships. One man said that he'd been to Saturn in a spaceship!

Did anyone else see that?

But we don't know if these stories are true.

2 What about the photographs that people say they have taken of alien spaceships?

The photos usually show oddly-shaped clouds or aeroplanes with the Sun shining on them.

3 Didn't people used to think that there could be aliens living on Mars?

Yes, but then space probes went to Mars. The photos they took didn't show any signs of alien life.

4 I heard that machines listening for messages picked up a clicking noise from space. Was that aliens trying to talk to us?

CLICK CLICK CLICK CLICK

Scientists found out that it was just a very noisy star.

5 Has anyone sent a message into space?

Yes, one spacecraft was sent into space carrying a greeting from countries all over Earth. But no one has replied yet.

Dear Aliens we are humans and we live here
Hello! Hello!
Earth
Solar System

STILL A MYSTERY

Nobody knows whether or not aliens exist. Maybe one day we'll find out or maybe we'll just never know...

Fast facts

Here, you can find out amazing facts about the planets in our solar system.

This picture shows the planets in order from the Sun. Underneath, there's the size of each planet, measured around its middle.

Mercury

Big or small: small
Surface: hard and rocky
Hot or cold: scorching hot during the day but freezing cold at night.
Interesting fact: Mercury is covered with thousands of rocky craters.
Moons: 0

Venus

Big or small: medium-sized
Surface: hard and rocky with lots of mountains.
Hot or cold: sizzling hot
Interesting fact: Venus is the hottest planet of all. It's hotter than the inside of an oven.
Moons: 0

Earth

Big or small: medium-sized
Surface: rocky
Hot or cold: not too hot or too cold. It's just right for life to exist.
Interesting fact: the Earth is the only planet with air, oceans and living things.
Moons: 1

Mars

Big or small: small – less than half the size of Earth.
Surface: rocky
Hot or cold: very cold
Interesting fact: Mars is a frozen desert covered with old volcanoes.
Moons: 2

Jupiter

Big or small: gigantic
Surface: soft and cloudy, with a rocky middle.
Hot or cold: freezing cold
Interesting fact: Jupiter is the biggest planet in our solar system. It's so huge that all the other planets in the solar system could fit inside it.
Moons: at least 16

n

Mercury	Venus	Earth	Mars	Jupiter	Saturn	Uranus	Neptune	Pluto
4,878 kilometres	12,104 kilometres	12,756 kilometres	6,796 kilometres	142,984 kilometres	120,536 kilometres	51,118 kilometres	49,500 kilometres	2,300 kilometres

Saturn

Big or small: huge
Surface: soft and cloudy, with a rocky middle.
Hot or cold: freezing cold and very windy.
Interesting fact: Saturn's seven flat rings are made of millions of pieces of ice and rock.
Moons: at least 18

Uranus

Big or small: very big
Surface: soft and cloudy, with a hard middle.
Hot or cold: freezing cold
Interesting fact: Uranus is the only planet that travels round the Sun tipped on its side.
Moons: at least 15

Neptune

Big or small: very big
Surface: soft and cloudy, with a rocky middle.
Hot or cold: freezing cold
Interesting fact: there's a dark spot on Neptune. It's a huge storm that's even bigger than the Earth.
Moons: at least 8

Pluto

Big or small: tiny
Surface: rocky and probably covered in ice.
Hot or cold: freezing cold
Interesting fact: Pluto is the furthest planet from the Sun. It takes 248 Earth years to travel round the Sun once.
Moons: 1

Puzzles

Here are some puzzles to try. Look back in the book to help you find the answers.

Close-up!

We've zoomed in on some things in our solar system that you've seen earlier. Can you tell what they are?

Space journey

These rockets are flying to three different planets. Follow the lines to see where each rocket is going.

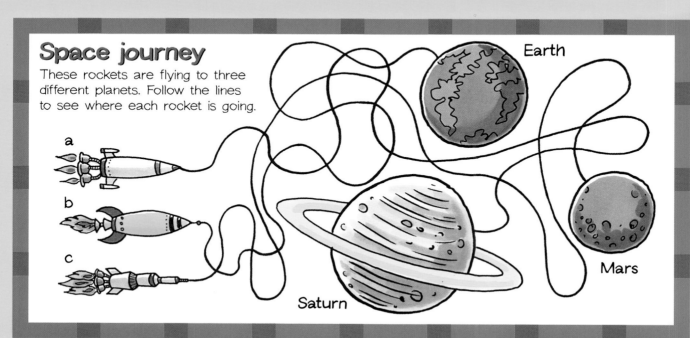

Earth

Mars

Saturn

a

b

c

Spot the difference

Look carefully at this astronaut standing on the Moon. Can you spot four differences between the pictures?

a

b

Pick and mix

Imagine you're an astronaut. Which three pieces of clothing would you choose to wear with your spacesuit?

Index

Created and published by
Two-Can Publishing Ltd
346 Old Street
London
EC1V 9RB

Consultant: Anthony Wilson
Main illustrations: John Egan, Eric Robson
Cartoon illustrations: Alan Rowe
Photographs: front cover John Egan;
p8 NOAA/Science Photo Library.

ISBN 1-85434-790-X

Dewey Decimal Classification 523.2

Paperback 10 9 8 7 6 5 4 3 2 1

A catalogue record for this book is available from the British Library.

Printed in Hong Kong by Wing King Tong